Mother & Daughter Tell-All Journal

by Tia S. Brown & Kylie C. Malone

ISBN# 978-1-7923-7088-5

This Journal Belongs To:

Hey Princess,

Waiting for you to get old enough to talk about everyday "girl things" was torture! I knew from the very beginning that you would be my guiding light even in my darkest hour.

As you got older, I could tell that you always wanted to tell me your secrets, but were nervous as to how I would react to some of the topics. I tried my best to make you feel comfortable with opening up to me, but I could tell that you were holding back.

Creating this journal was a way for us to communicate in a no-judgement zone. I want you to feel at ease sharing your deepest and darkest secrets, because my goal is to be able to help you though every obstacle you may encounter. Sharing my personal stories will help you make better choices, so here goes everything!

I love you more than you know Princess!

-Tia

Hey Ma,

I've been waiting patiently until I got old enough to tell you all about the secrets and stories I have kept hidden inside for so long.

I've always wanted to tell you my inner-most thoughts, but was nervous because I didn't know how you would react. As I got older, I realized that we both were comfortable enough to talk to each other about topics that may have been considered as "risky".

Creating this journal was a way for me to open up to you truthfully and whole-heartedly about the different bumps I have encountered so far on this road called life! I love the relationship we have now and it has a lot to do with our willingness to open up to one another without judgement.

I love you Ma!

-Kylie

Friendly Guide:

1. Remember that this journal is to be kept in a safe place at all times!
2. Each Princess page is labeled with a heart.
2. Be open to share without the fear of judgement!
3. Have FUN with your drawings! They are there to make the journal even more interesting!
4. Honesty is a requirement of this journal!
5. There are no wrong answers!

Loyalty + Homesty =
An Unbreakable Bond

DATE

Hey Ma,

What did you love to do most as a child?

DATE

Hey Princess,

What did you love to do most as a child?

HEY MA,

WHAT MADE YOU SMILE AS A KID?

(USE PICTURES OR WORDS)

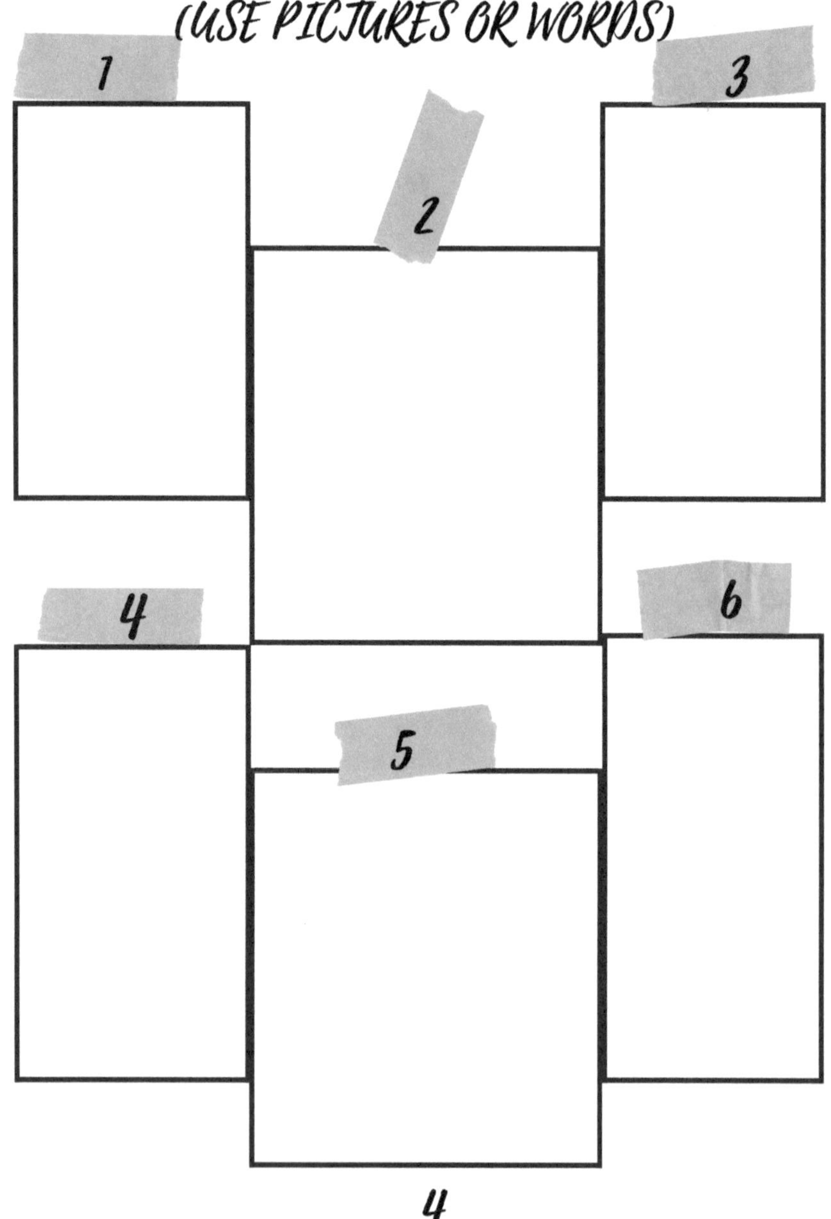

HEY PRINCESS,

WHAT MADE YOU SMILE AS A KID?

(USE PICTURES OR WORDS)

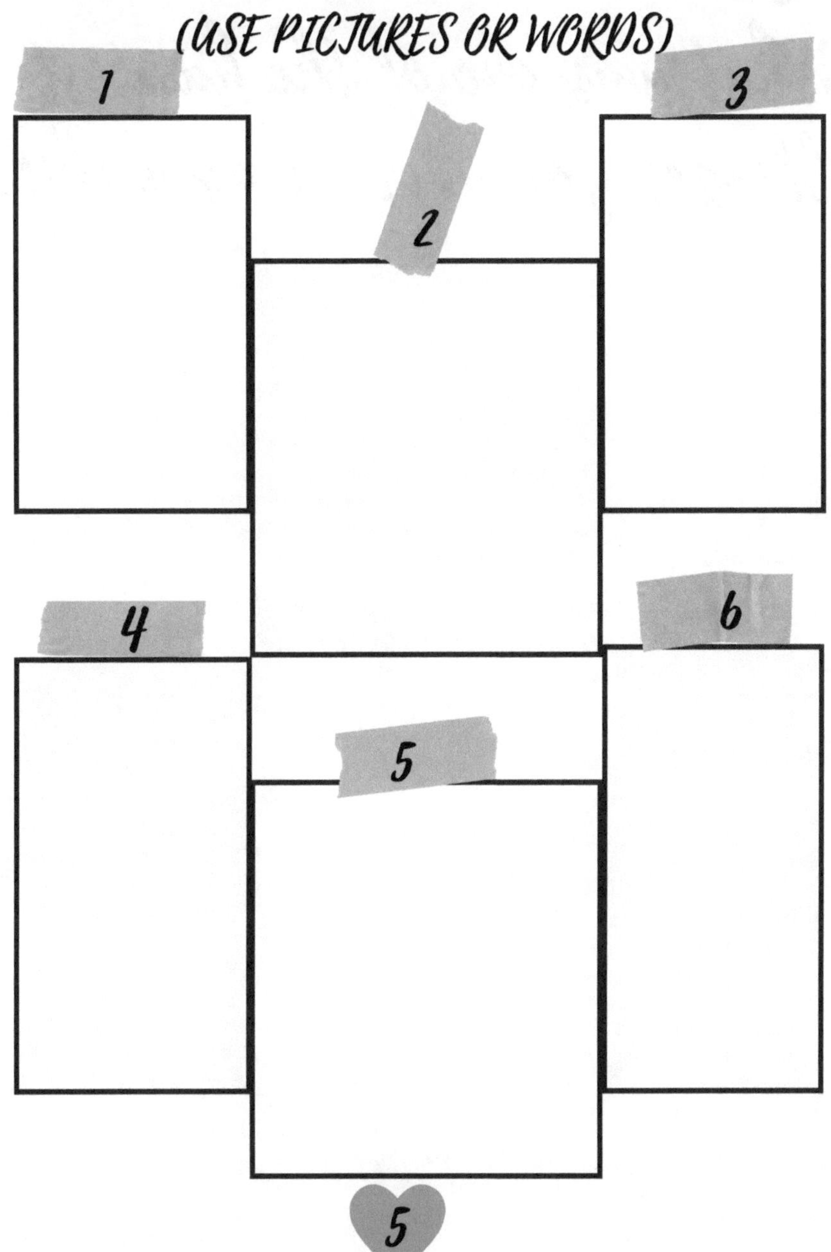

DATE

Hey Ma,

What was one of the hardest challenges you overcme as a child?

DATE

Hey Princess,

What was one of the hardest challenges you overcame so far?

Hey Ma,

What did you look like as a child?

(Draw or tape pictures)

Hey Princess,

What were your favorite pictures from your childhood?

DATE

Hey Ma,

What was the most dangerous thing you did as a child?

DATE

Hey Princess,

What was the most dangerous thing you did as a child?

DATE

Hey Ma,

What was the sadest moment of your childhood?

(Draw a picture of how you felt.)

DATE

Hey Princess,

What was the sadest moment of your childhood?

(Draw a picture of how you felt.)

DATE

Hey Ma

How would you describe your personality as a teen?

DATE

Hey Princess,

How would you describe your personality as a teen?

DATE

Hey Ma,

What were your top 10 songs as a child?

1. ____________
2. ____________
3. ____________
4. ____________
5. ____________
6. ____________
7. ____________
8. ____________
9. ____________
10. ____________

DATE

Hey Princess,

What were your top 10 songs as a child?

1. ____________
2. ____________
3. ____________
4. ____________
5. ____________
6. ____________
7. ____________
8. ____________
9. ____________
10. ____________

DATE

Hey Ma,

What is your favorite song now?

(Write the lyrics to your favorite part.)

Song Name: ______________________

DATE

Hey Princess,

What is your favorite song now?

(Write the lyrics to your favorite part.)

Song Name: ______________________

DATE

Hey Ma,

What were your top 10 movies growing up?

1. ____________
6. ____________
2. ____________
7. ____________
3. ____________
8. ____________
4. ____________
9. ____________
5. ____________
10. ____________

DATE

Hey Princess,

What are your top 10 movies?

1. ____________
2. ____________
3. ____________
4. ____________
5. ____________
6. ______________
7. ______________
8. ______________
9. ______________
10. ______________

DATE

Hey Ma,

What is your favorite movie now?
(Who is your favorite character and why?)

Movie Name: ___________________________

Actor/Actress: _________________________

DATE

Hey Princess,

What is your favorite movie now?
(Who is your favorite character and why?)

Movie Name: ______________________

Actor/Actress: ______________________

DATE

Hey Ma,

What words would you use to describe me?

(Write 1 word for each point.)

DATE

Hey Princess,

What words would you use to describe me?

(Write 1 word for each point.)

DATE

Hey Ma,

Draw or write anything your heart desires.

DATE

Hey Princess,

Draw or write anything your heart desires.

HEY MA,

WHAT DO YOU LIKE TO DO TO RELAX?

(USE PICTURES OR WORDS)

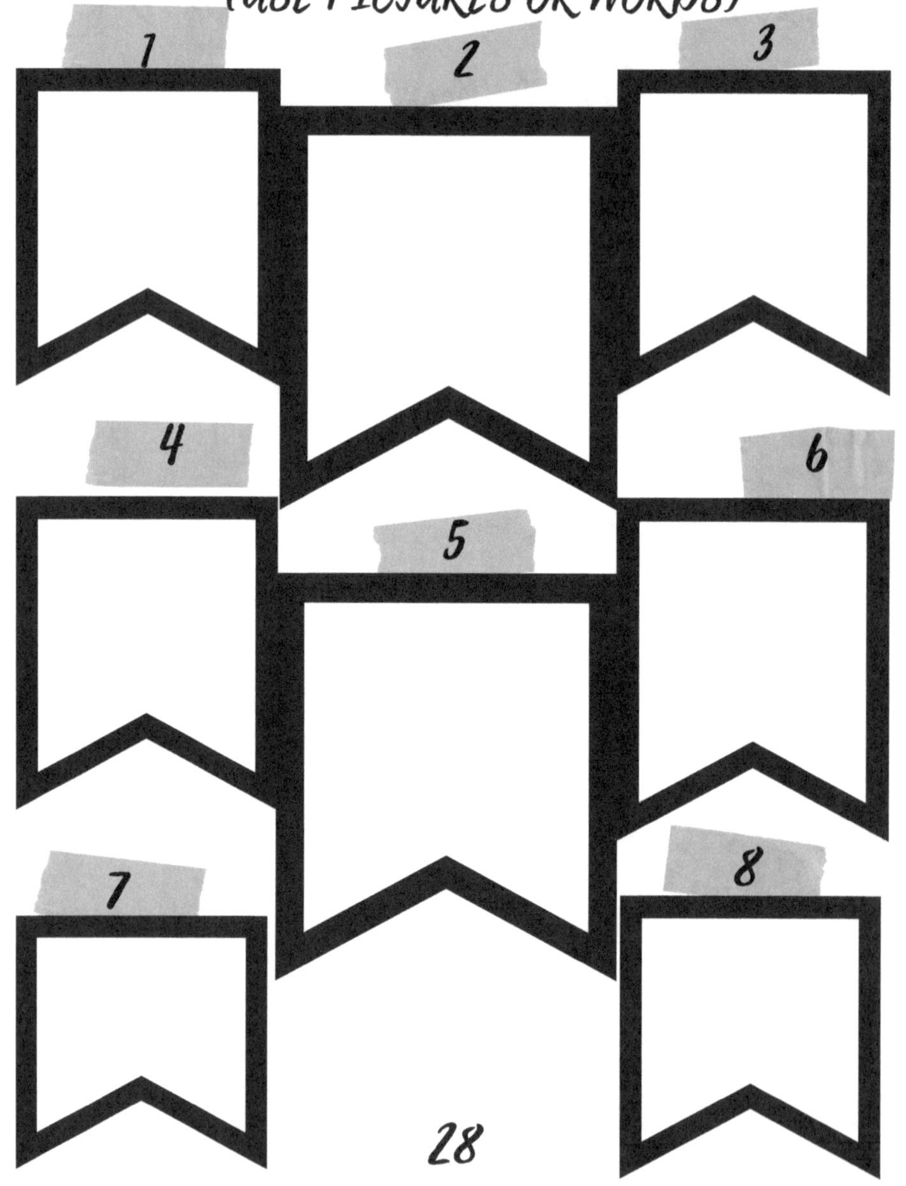

HEY PRINCESS,

WHAT DO YOU LIKE TO DO TO RELAX?

(USE PICTURES OR WORDS)

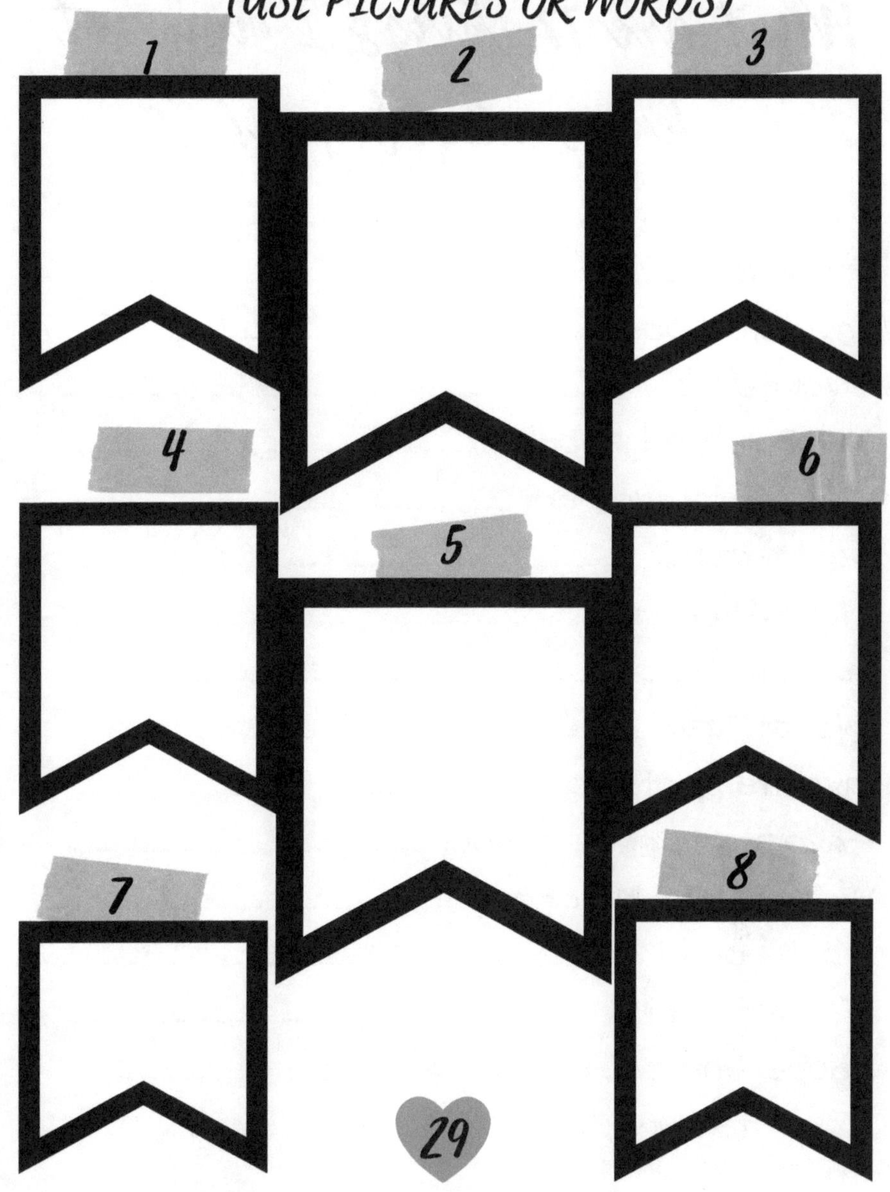

DATE

Hey Ma,

What are 17 things I may not know about you?

1. Favorite color: ______________________
2. Favorite Actor/Actress: ______________
3. Favorite food: ______________________
4.Favorite book: ______________________
5. Most disliked food:__________________
6. Weird thing you do: _________________
7. Best friend: _________________________
8. Worst friend: ______________________
9. Favorite Trip: _______________________
10. Worst Trip: ________________________
11. Favorite quote: _____________________
12. Favorite year in school: _____________
13. Worst year in school: _______________
14. Last food I ate: ____________________
15. Favorite drink: _____________________
16. I hope for: ________________________
17. Favorite thing to do with me: __________

DATE

Hey Princess,

What are 17 things I may not know about you?

1. Favorite color: ______________________
2. Favorite Actor/Actress: ______________
3. Favorite food: ______________________
4. Favorite book: ______________________
5. Most disliked food: __________________
6. Weird thing you do: _________________
7. Best friend: ________________________
8. Worst friend: _______________________
9. Favorite Trip: ______________________
10. Worst Trip: ________________________
11. Favorite quote: ____________________
12. Favorite year in school: _____________
13. Worst year in school: _______________
14. Last food I ate: ____________________
15. Favorite drink: _____________________
16. I hope for: ________________________
17. Favorite thing to do with me: _________

DATE

Hey Ma,

How did you stay active as a child?
Draw or tape 3 pictures.

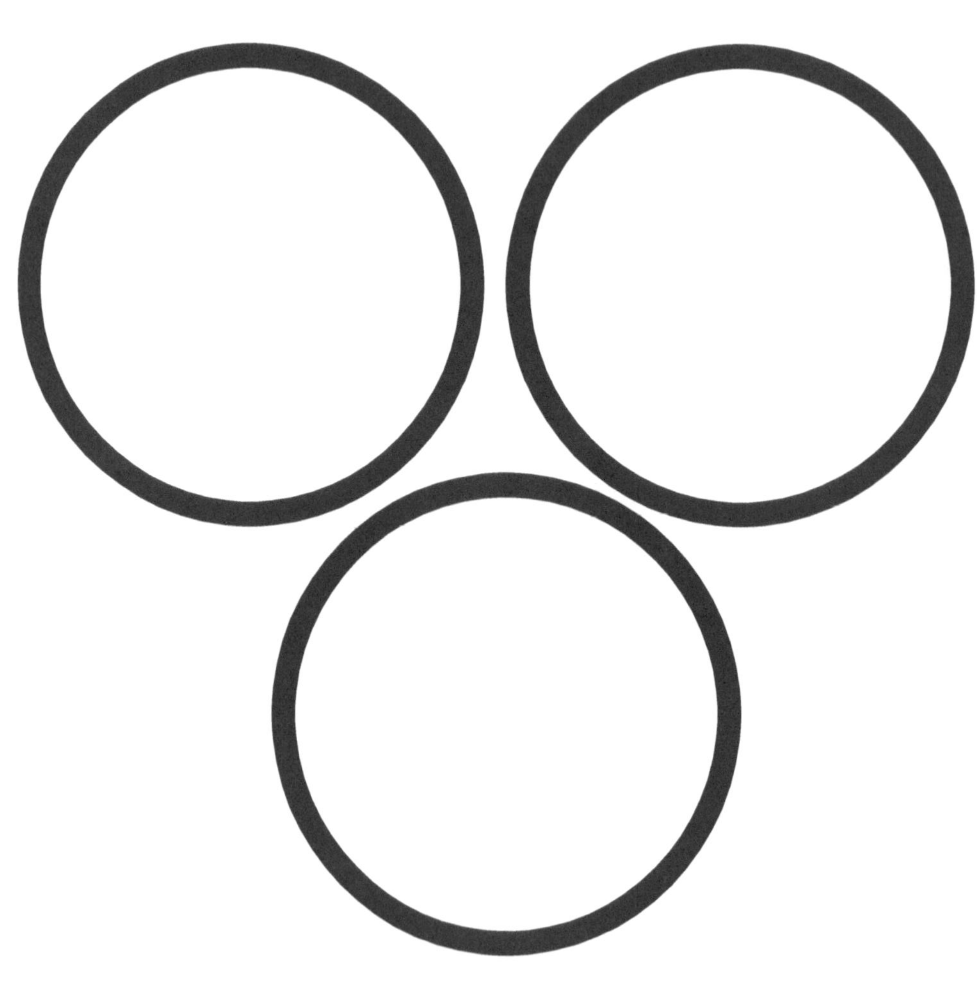

DATE

Hey Princess,

How did you stay active as a child?

Draw or tape 3 pictures.

DATE

Hey Ma,

What did you want to be when you grew up?

DATE

Hey Princess,

What d0 you want to be when you grew up?

DATE

Hey Ma,

What do you believe?

(Free write or bullet)

DATE

Hey Princess,

What do you believe?
(Free write or bullet)

DATE

Hey Ma,

What are 7 qualities you look for in a bestfriend?

Draw or write in each shape.

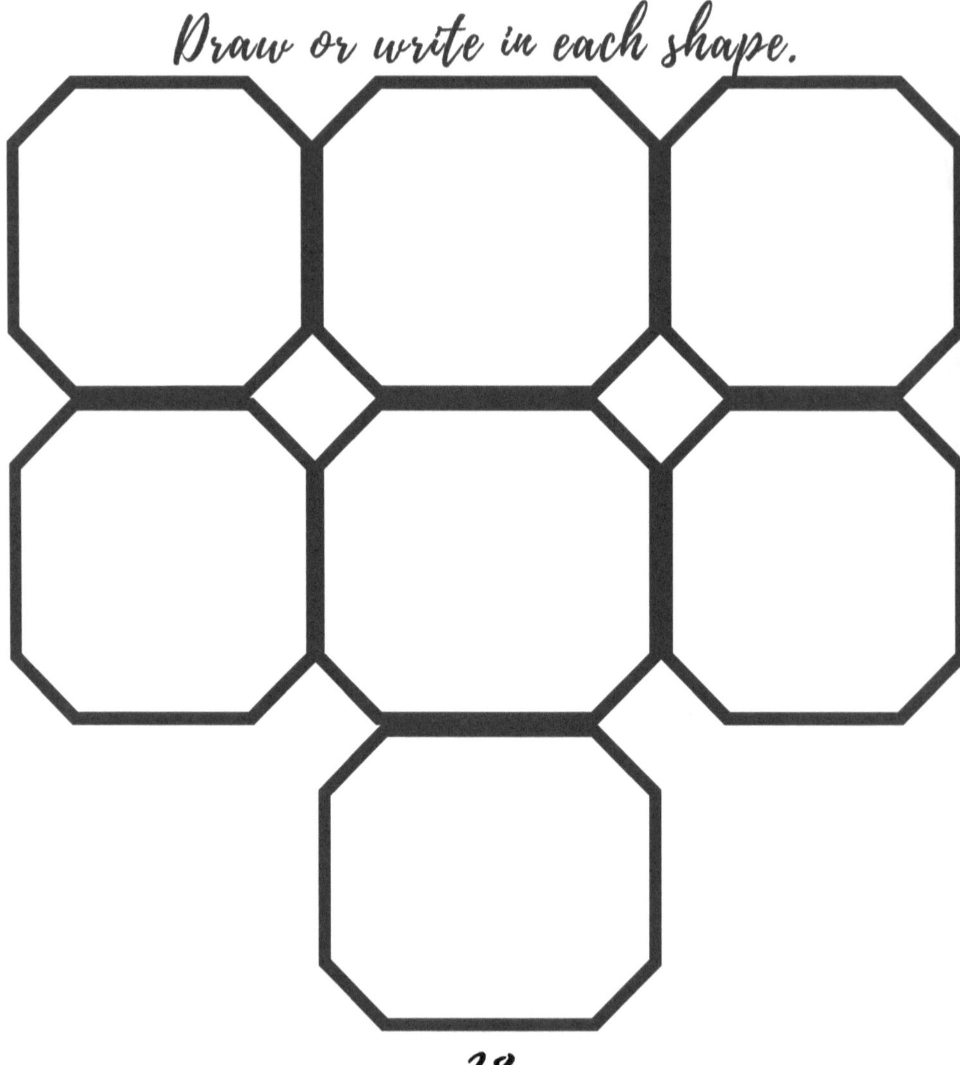

DATE

Hey Princess,

What are 7 qualities you look for in a bestfriend?

Draw or write in each shape.

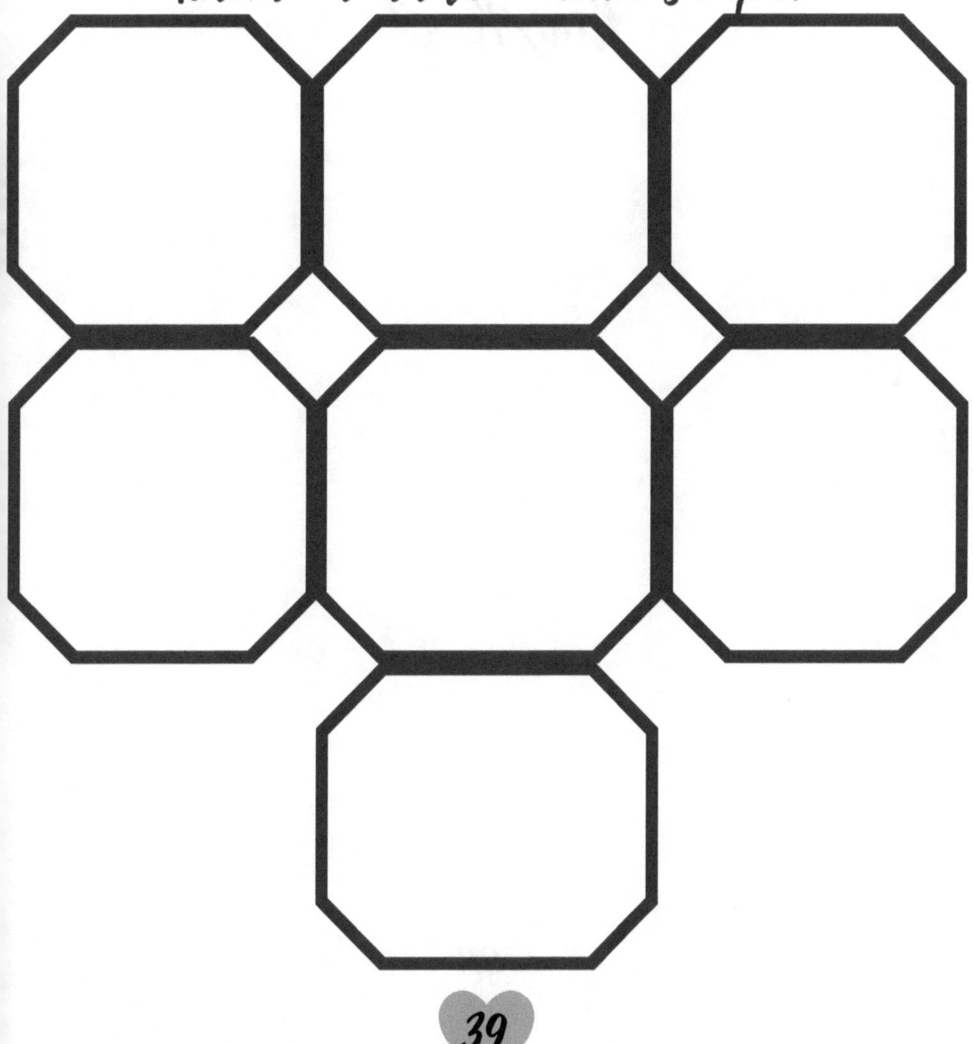

DATE

Hey Ma,

Who was your bestfriend as a child? Why did you choose him/her?

DATE

Hey Princess,

Who was your bestfriend as a child? Why did you choose him/her?

DATE

Hey Ma,

What friend did you find out was dead weight in your life? Why?

(Draw or tape a picture.)

Name: ________________________

DATE

Hey Princess,

What friend did you find out was dead weight in your life? Why?

(Draw or tape a picture.)

Name: ______________________

DATE

Hey Ma,

What was your favorite childhood trip? Why?

(Draw or tape a picture.)

DATE

Hey Princess,

What was your favorite childhood trip? Why?

(Draw or tape a picture.)

DATE

Hey Ma,

What do you love the most about me?

DATE

Hey Princess,

What do you love the most about me?

DATE

Hey Ma,

Draw a picture of the best birthday you had as a child!

DATE

Hey Princess,

Draw a picture of the best birthday you had as a child!

DATE

Hey Ma,

If you could tell me something else about you that I don't know, what would it be?

DATE

Hey Princess,

If you could tell me something else about you that I don't know, what would it be?

DISCLAIMER

Unless otherwise indicated, all the names, characters, places, events and incidents in this journal are the product of the author's real life and must be treated with the utmost secrecy.
As you share some of your innermost thoughts secrets, laughs and a few tears, know that the bond you are building with each other is unbreakable!

Take a deep breathe and dive in!

-Tia & Kylie

DATE

Hey Ma,

What went through your head when you found out you were pregnant?

DATE

Hey Princess,

Do you want to have children? Why or why not?

HEY MA,

WHICH 8 EXPERIENCES WILL YOU NEVER FORGET?

(USE PICTURES OR WORDS)

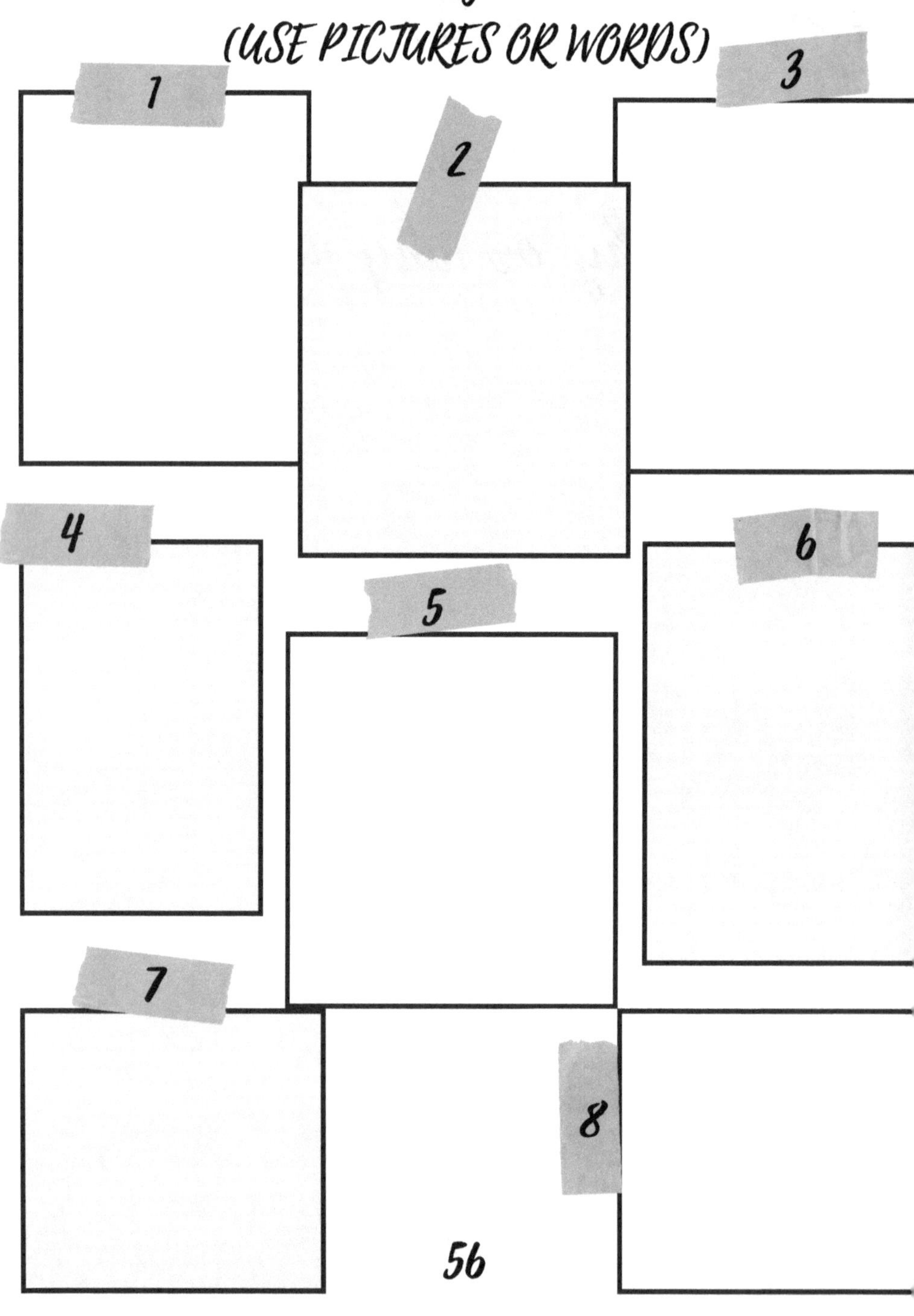

HEY PRINCESS,

WHICH 8 EXPERIENCES WILL YOU NEVER FORGET?

(USE PICTURES OR WORDS)

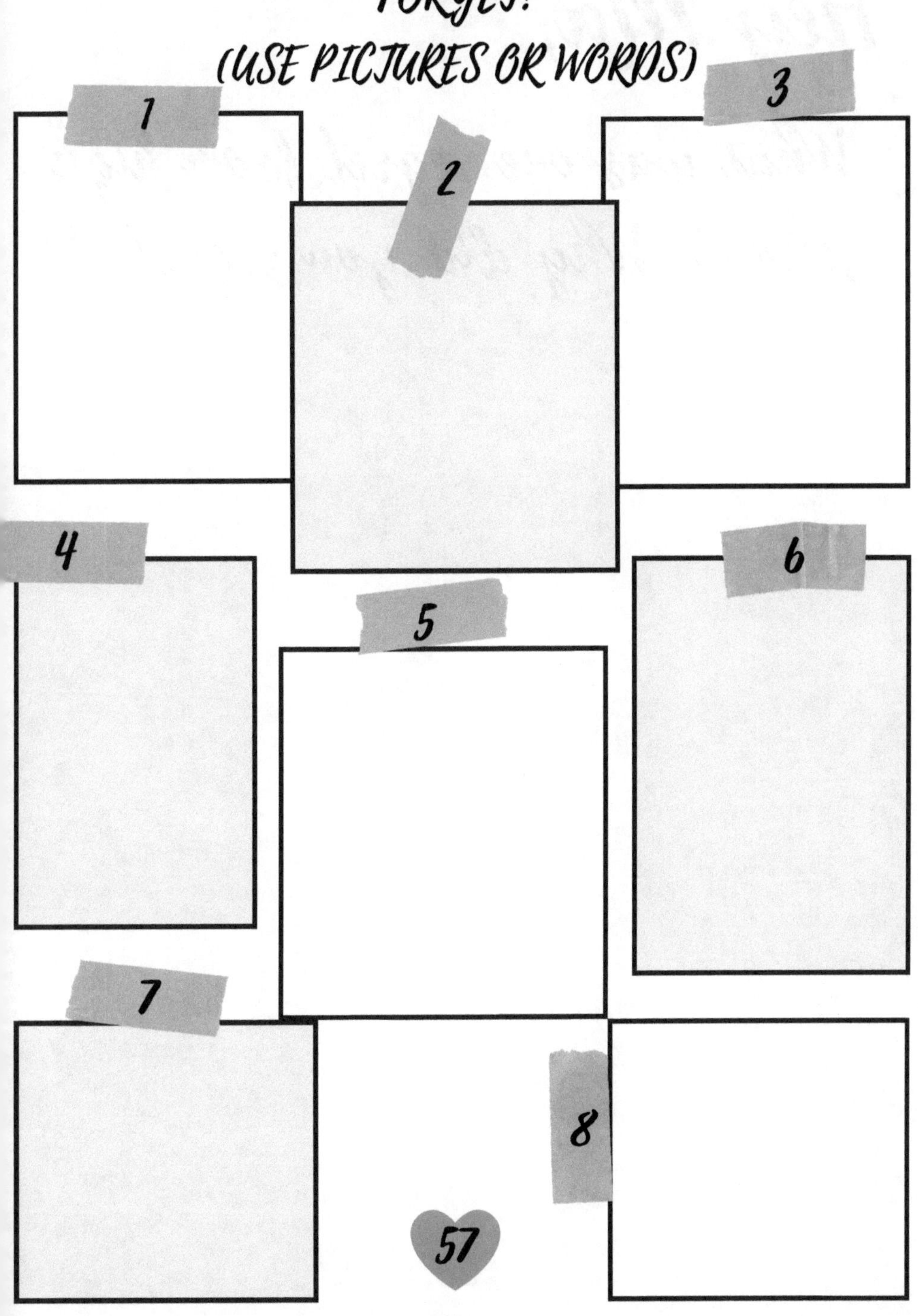

DATE

Hey Ma,

What was one regret from high school? Why did you regret it?

DATE

Hey Princess,

What was one regret from high school? Why did you regret it?

Hey Ma,

What were your 2 worst fears?

(Draw or tape pictures)

Hey Princess,

What were your 2 worst fears?

(Draw or tape pictures)

DATE

Hey Ma,

What was your first experience in a relationship like?

DATE

Hey Princess,

What was your first experience in a relationship like?

DATE

Hey Ma,

How did your first crush look?

(Draw a picture of how your crush looked.)

DATE

Hey Princess,

How did your first crush look?

(Draw a picture of how your crush looked.)

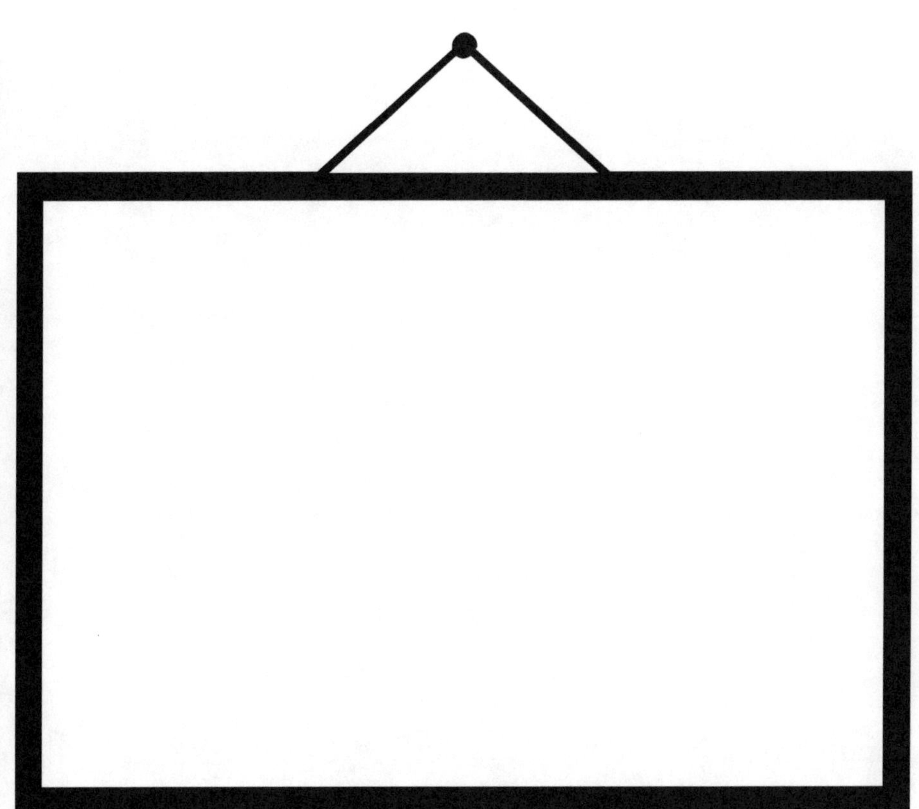

DATE

Hey Ma,

How did you know that you had feelings for your first crush?

DATE

Hey Princess,

How did you know that you had feelings for your first crush?

DATE

Hey Ma,

What were your top 10 favorite things to say as a teen?

1. ______________ 6. ______________

2. ______________ 7. ______________

3. ______________ 8. ______________

4. ______________ 9. ______________

5. ______________ 10. ______________

DATE

Hey Princess,

What are your top 10 favorite things to say?

1. ______________ 6. ______________

2. ______________ 7. ______________

3. ______________ 8. ______________

4. ______________ 9. ______________

5. ______________ 10. ______________

DATE

Hey Ma,

What was your first kiss like? How did you feel?

DATE

Hey Princess,

What was your first kiss like? If the day has not come yet, how do you think you will feel?

DATE

Hey Ma,

What are 10 things you can see yourself doing for the rest of your life

1. ______________ 6. ______________

2. ______________ 7. ______________

3. ______________ 8. ______________

4. ______________ 9. ______________

5. ______________ 10. ______________

DATE

Hey Princess,

What are 10 things you can see yourself doing for the rest of your life?

1. ______________ 6. ______________

2. ______________ 7. ______________

3. ______________ 8. ______________

4. ______________ 9. ______________

5. ______________ 10. ______________

DATE

Hey Ma,

What was the worst situation you were in as a teen? What did you do?

DATE

Hey Princess,

What was the worst situation you were in as a teen? What did you do?

DATE

Hey Ma,

What words would you use to describe yourself as a teen?

(Write 1 word for each point.)

DATE

Hey Princess,

What words would you use to describe yourself as a teen?

(Write 1 word for each point.)

DATE

Hey Ma,

Draw or write anything your heart desires.

DATE

Hey Princess,

Draw or write anything your heart desires.

HEY MA,

WHO WERE THE MOST IMPORTANT PEOPLE IN YOUR LIFE?

(USE PICTURES OR WORDS)

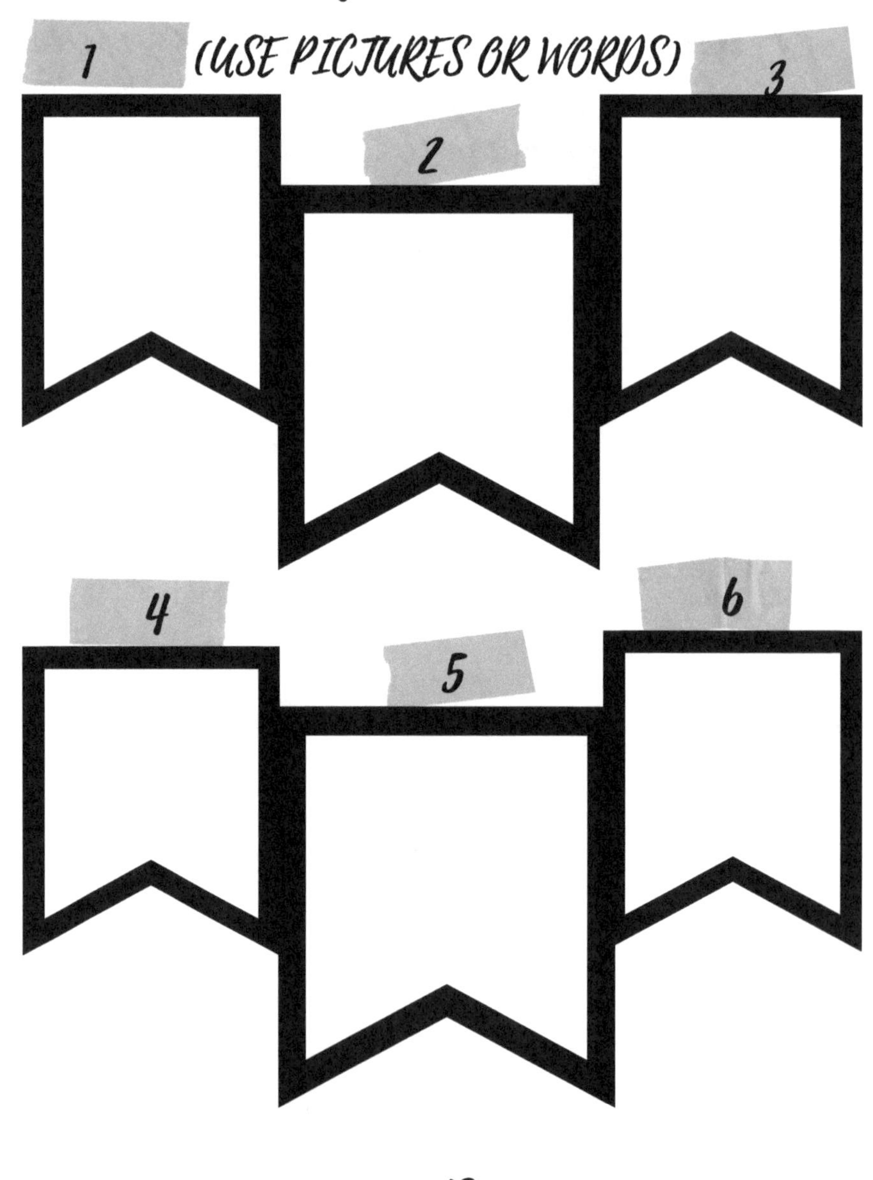

HEY PRINCESS,

WHO WERE THE MOST IMPORTANT PEOPLE IN YOUR LIFE?

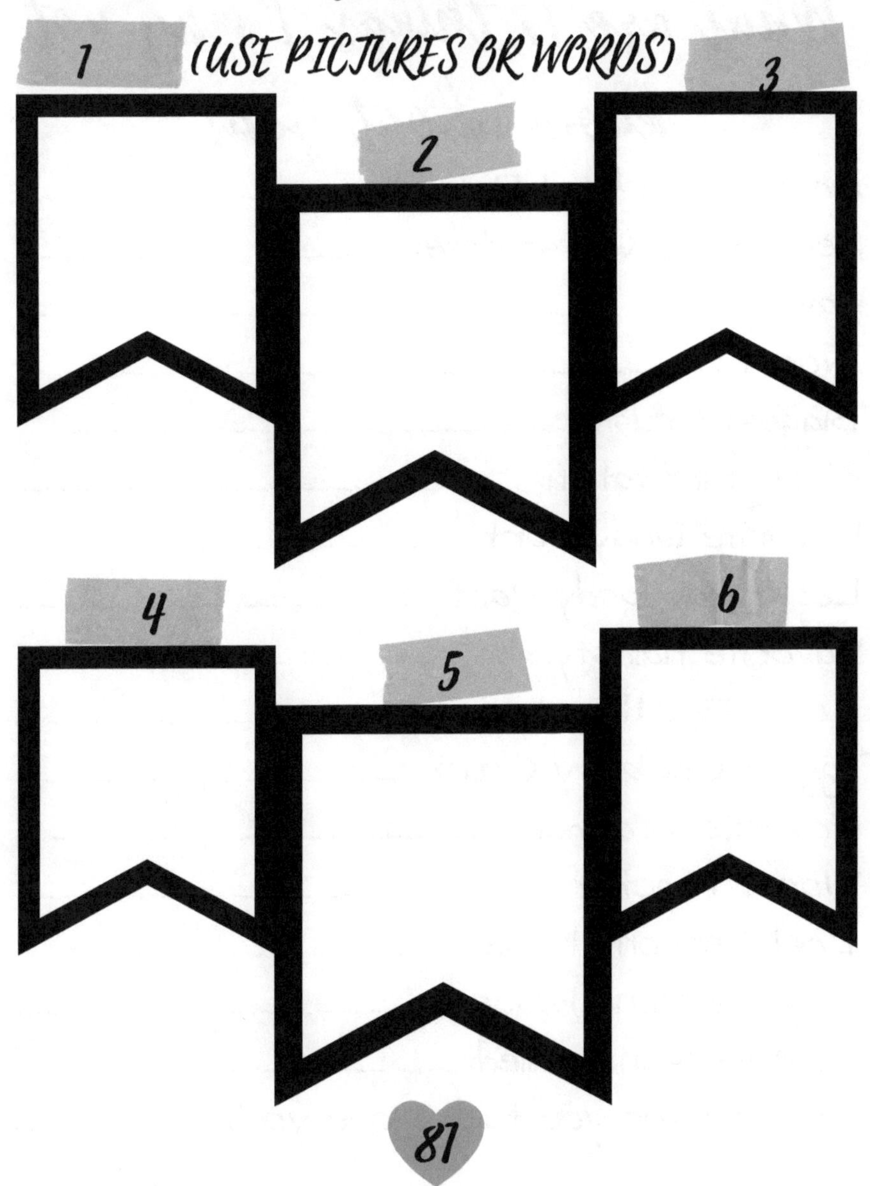

DATE

Hey Ma,

What are 17 things I may not know about you?

1. Idea of a perfect Date: _______________
2. Idea of the worst date: _______________
3. Favorite Ex: _______________________
4. Worst Ex: ________________________
5. Biggest Crush:______________________
6. Biggest Irritation: __________________
7. Favorite Body Part: _________________
8. Least Fav Body Part: ________________
9. Favorite Hairstyle: _________________
10. Least Fav Hairstyle: ________________
11. Biggest Celebrity Crush: _____________
12. Favorite Teacher: __________________
13. Worst Teacher: ____________________
14. Last Person I kissed: ________________
15. Last Person I hugged: _______________
16. Last Person I called: ________________
17. Last person you told, "I love you": _______

DATE

Hey Princess,

What are 17 things I may not know about you?

1.1. Idea of a perfect Date: ________________

2. Idea of the worst date: _______________

3. Favorite Ex: ________________________

4. Worst Ex: __________________________

5. Biggest Crush:_______________________

6. Biggest Irritation: ____________________

7. Favorite Body Part: __________________

8. Least Fav Body Part: _________________

9. Favorite Hairstyle: ___________________

10. Least Fav Hairstyle: __________________

11. Biggest Celebrity Crush: ______________

12. Favorite Teacher: ____________________

13. Worst Teacher: ______________________

14. Last Person I kissed: _________________

15. Last Person I hugged: _________________

16. Last Person I called: __________________

17. Last person you told, "I love you": ___________

DATE

Hey Ma,

What are 3 personal flaws you want to work on?

Draw or write.

DATE

Hey Princess,

What are 3 personal flaws you want to work on?

Draw or write.

DATE

Hey Ma,

Do you think you were a leader or follower as a teen? Why?

DATE

Hey Princess,

Do you think you are a leader or follower? Why?

DATE

Hey Ma,

At what moment were you the most proud of me?

(Free write or bullet)

DATE

Hey Princess,

At what moment were you the most proud of me?

(Free write or bullet)

DATE

Hey Ma,

What are 7 obstacles you overcame that you thought you couldn't?

Draw or write in each shape.

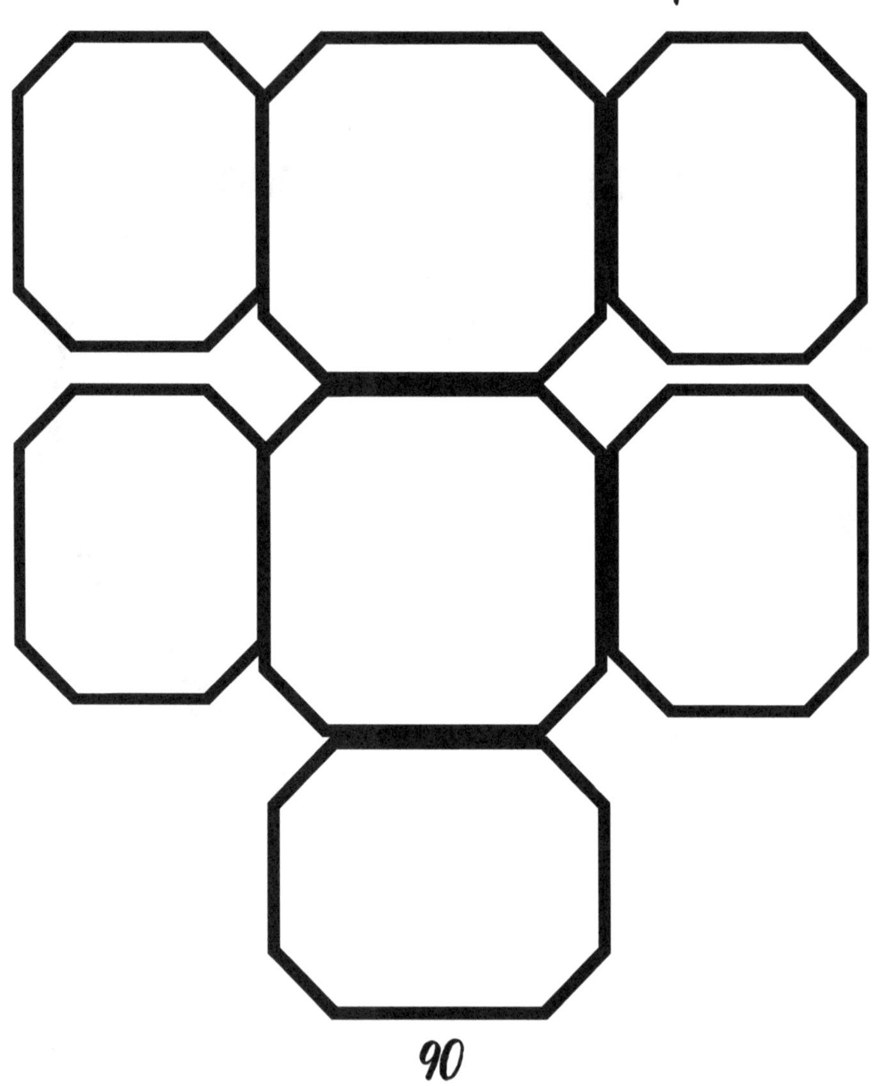

DATE

Hey Princess,

What are 7 obstacles you overcame that you thought you couldn't?

Draw or write in each shape.

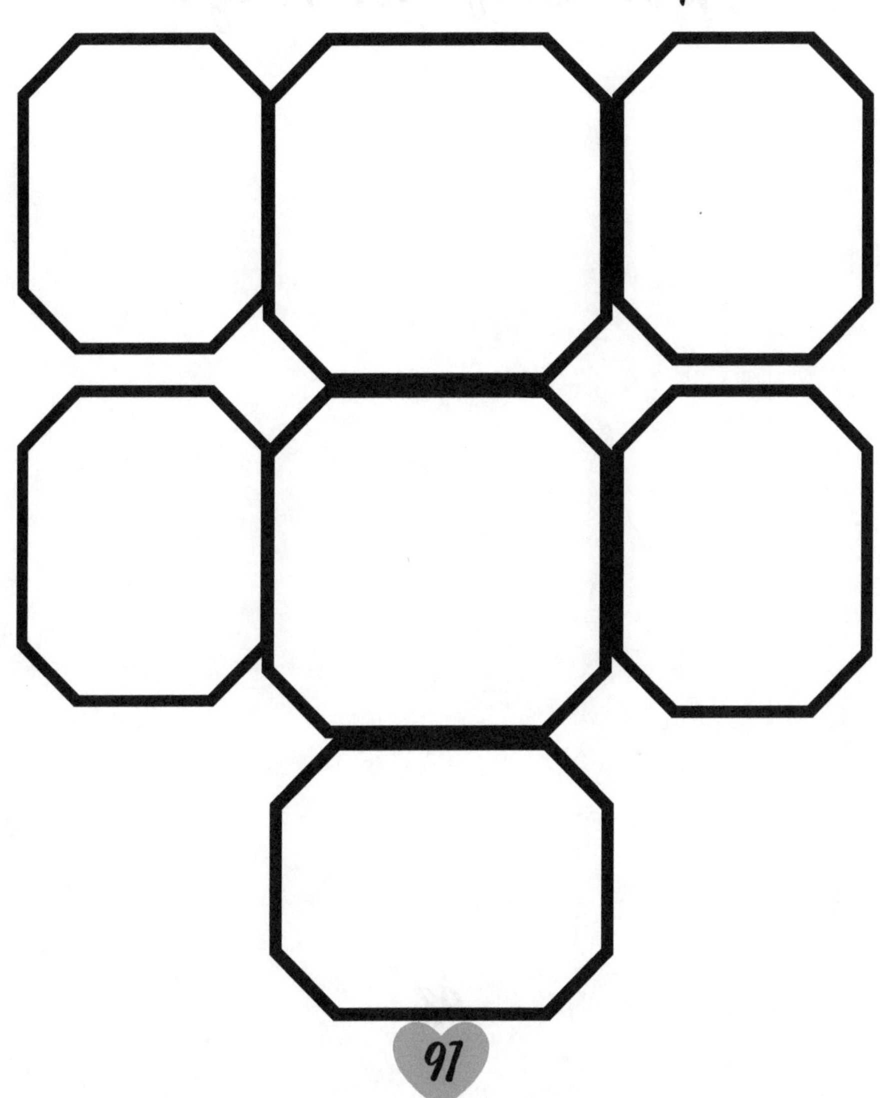

DATE

Hey Ma,

At what moment were you least proud of me? Why?

DATE

Hey Princess,

At what moment were you least proud of me? Why?

Hey Ma,

DATE

When was a time that you stood up for yourself? How did you feel?

(Draw or tape a picture.)

Feeling: ______________________

Hey Princess,

DATE

When was a time that you stood up for yourself? How did you feel?

(Draw or tape a picture.)

Feeling: ______________________

Hey Ma,

DATE

If you could travel anywhere, where would you go? Why?

(Draw or tape a picture.)

Hey Princess,

DATE

If you could travel anywhere, where would you go? Why?

(Draw or tape a picture.)

DATE

Hey Ma,

Did your Mom talk to you about dating? What was that conversation like?

DATE

Hey Princess,

Do you have any additional questions about dating that you want me to answer?

DATE

Hey Ma,

Draw a picture of the worst birthday you had as a child!

Why was it the worst?

DATE

Hey Princess,

Draw a picture of the worst birthday you had as a child!

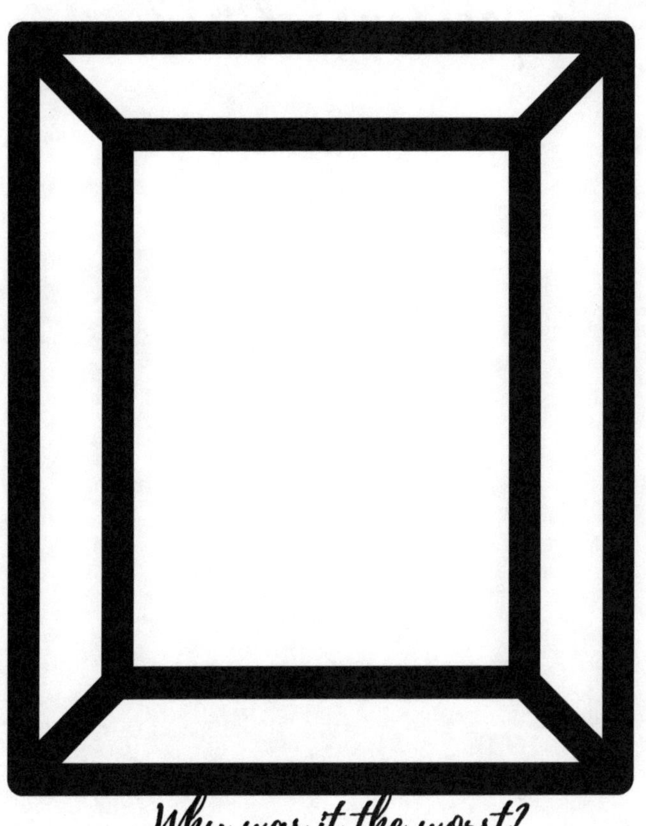

Why was it the worst?

DATE

Hey Ma,

What was your first sexual experience like?

DATE

Hey Princess,

What was your first sexual experience like or what do you anticipate? Why?

Thank you for joining us on this journey. We hope this experience was what your relationship needed to blossom!

Made in United States
Troutdale, OR
04/21/2024

19348682R10066